The Keys to the
Effortless Golf Swing

The Keys
to the Effortless
Golf Swing
Curing Your Hit Impulse
in Seven Simple Lessons

Michael McTeigue
PGA Teaching Professional

Library of Congress Cataloging-in-Publication Data
McTeigue, Michael.
    The keys to the effortless golf swing.
    Bibliography: p.

    1. Swing (Golf)   I. Title.
GV979.S9M34   1985   796.352'3   85-47661
ISBN 0-689-11630-6

10 9 8 7 6 5

Designed by Cathryn S. Aison

Printed in the United States of America

WITH LOVE AND AFFECTION
TO JIM AND TERRI
AND
JIM AND TERRI

Foreword

Most golf instruction books are written by famous performers about how they personally swing the club, and there's no doubt the better ones can be helpful—especially if you share the author's athleticism, ambition, appetite for work, and opportunities for practice and play.

This book was written by a very bright but at the time "unfamous" young teacher whose daily bread depended on delivering permanently decent-to-good golf games to averagely endowed people with no interest in becoming slaves to the sport. He became so successful at that in his immediate community that his pupils demanded he put the system on paper for their constant reference and reminder. He called the result *The Keys to the Effortless Golf Swing* and sent it to a number of star players, one of whom passed it on to me. After one quick reading I believed that the book would help so many other existing and would-be golfers to such an extent that it just had to be made available nationally. Jim McQueen, one of the world's top golf artists and a former professional, fully shared those sentiments and agreed to do the illustrations, and the nation's leading golf book publisher became an enthusiastic third party.

The key to Michael McTeigue's success with his thousands of pupils of all sizes, shapes, ages, and ability levels in California, and the beauty of this book, is the clarity and simplicity and the supremely logical *sequentiality* of its approach to the golf swing.

Follow the easily mastered steps or "keys" in the recommended order and with a reasonable degree of patience, and in a remarkably short time, you will be experiencing entirely new sensations of both accurate striking and effortless power. Encouraged by those— and the accompanying evaporation of confusion—you will persist with these simple and clear-cut moves until they become thoroughly muscle-memorized. At that point, you will be swinging the golf club effectively and with total confidence on every shot *entirely by feel,* which is the closest you or anyone else will ever come to golf's "secret" (ask any champion if you doubt that). Gone forever at long last will be the Band-Aids and the gimmicks and all that frustrating stumbling from one fruitless theory to another.

If you love golf and want to play better for a lot less effort, then forget Michael McTeigue's fame quotient and work with this little gem of a book. It could make you as big a fan of his as all those happy pupils for whom he originally wrote it.

Ken Bowden
May, 1985

A former editorial director of Golf Digest *magazine, Ken Bowden has coauthored more than a dozen golf instruction books, seven of them with Jack Nicklaus.*

Acknowledgments

Few of the ideas presented here were born of my imagination; most of them were first offered in some similar vein by someone else. Thus the value of this manuscript, I believe, lies in its synthesis and simplification of a host of useful ideas about the golf swing.

The great players, teachers, writers, and illustrators listed below represent a tremendous range of opinion about the game and the swing. Each person's approach has broadened my view, stimulated my thinking, and contributed significantly to the success my students have enjoyed. I am grateful for their willingness to share their views in their writings, and, in some cases, in person with me.

So, my thanks to Tommy Armour, Dick Aultman, Jimmy Ballard, Percy Boomer, Ken Bowden, Pat Chartrand, Alastair Cochran and John Stobbs, Larry Dennis, Jack Doss, Jim Flick, Al Geiberger, Ben Hogan, John Jacobs, Bobby Jones, Jim McQueen, Dale Mead, Johnny Miller, Michael Murphy, Eddie Merrins, Byron Nelson, Jack Nicklaus, Joe Novak, Gary Player, Anthony Ravielli, Ron Rhoads, Paul Runyan, Sam Snead, Bob Toski, Lee Trevino, Ken Venturi, Gary Wiren... and the other players and pros who have shared their ideas with me.

My deepest appreciation goes to Ken Bowden, my editor, whose interest, guidance, and editorial expertise made this little book a reality. It has been both a thrill and an education to work with Ken, his wife Jean, and with our talented illustrator, Jim McQueen. Many thanks also to JoAnn Jonson for her timely assistance in processing the text.

Contents

The Keys to the
Effortless Golf Swing

Before We Begin...

My purpose in writing *The Keys to the Effortless Golf Swing* is to enable you, the reader, to generate greater swing power, and hit the golf ball farther and straighter than ever before, with the feeling and look of great ease.

This we will accomplish by building the ideal sequence of body motions during the swing. Our task will be much easier than you might imagine.

During my many hours on the lesson tee, students have often remarked: "My practice swing is so easy and smooth, yet the moment I put a ball there, I feel like I'm chopping wood. Why is that?" Well, let's consider our intent in both cases. During practice swings, our intent is to feel relaxed, to sense good rhythm, and to swing to a nice full finish. With a ball before us, our intent becomes to strike the ball, to hit it with great force. The swing is no longer "timed" to the finish, but to the ball position. So, inevitably, the two swings feel completely different.

"Building the ideal sequence of body motions will be much easier than you might imagine."

Thus it may be that the single greatest cause of poor golf shots is the player's mental image of the clubhead striking the ball. This image, coupled with our intent to *hit* the ball, forces us to attack the ball and thereby destroys the ideal sequence of body motion. Helping you overcome this hit instinct, and creating and maintaining the ideal sequence of motion in your swing, is the major theme and objective of this book.

Before presenting the keys to the effortless swing, I must introduce five basic concepts about the creation of golf shots. We utilize three of these concepts immediately as we begin building the effortless swing. The fourth and fifth concepts become invaluable when you take your new swing to the golf course.

These five basic concepts are:

1. Relax.
2. Play by feel.
3. Swing, don't hit.
4. Say yea (positive expectancy).
5. Visualize.

Let's look briefly at each of them.

Relaxation

Please stand up and stiffen every muscle in your body. Stay as tensed as you can and try to hurry across the room. Chances are you did not get very far very fast. The reason is simple: Tensed muscles inhibit motion. A relaxed muscle moves faster than a tensed one.

The vast majority of bad swings result from excess tension in the hands, arms, shoulders, and back. We will discuss this in more detail later, but, for now, I would rather have your upper body much too relaxed than much too tense. You can always increase the muscle tension slightly to support the club if you get too relaxed, but this is rarely a problem.

Players who have difficulty relaxing should stiffen

the muscles in question for five to ten seconds, then relax them. Doing this several times will achieve an excellent state of relaxed readiness in the upper-body muscles.

Relaxation also applies to the player's mental attitude. Remaining calm and at ease, regardless of the myriad of tortures the game routinely inflicts upon us, increases our chances of thinking clearly and experiencing the proper sequence of motions in the swing. To paraphrase Sam Snead, if you must get angry, get "cool mad." Otherwise, take Walter Hagen's advice and "stop and smell the flowers along the way."

Play by Feel

Most average players prepare for a golf shot by counting down a mental checklist of setup and swing instructions. Some examples are: eye on the ball, left arm straight, shift weight, head steady. If the resulting swing fails to deliver the hoped-for shot, most players will analyze what they "did wrong," and then add one more instruction to the checklist. The result is a lengthy sequence of verbal mental commands, often changing from shot to shot, in a never-ending search for consistency.

At some point, we must abandon this constant, futile search and settle with some permanency on certain swing keys. These are the keys I will offer you. However, as soon as possible we want to leave the arena of verbal mental command and enter the realm of playing by feel. Imagine for a moment how it feels to put on a jacket and button it up, or climb a familiar flight of stairs. You are experiencing a sequence of remembered physical feelings, or kinesthetic sensations.

One remembered sensation can replace several verbal commands in the golf swing. The ultimate goal, then, is to learn to remember how a good swing feels, and anticipate or recreate that feeling right before the upcoming swing. Instead of counting down a lengthy checklist, the mind remains relatively silent while the body anticipates the proper feeling of the upcoming swing.

As we build the effortless swing, we will of necessity discuss specific body positions and movements. As soon as possible, however, these checkpoints will be translated into the realm of "feel." Your keys will become a sequence of familiar sensations, and you will be "playing by feel." Should you hit a bad shot, you will not analyze what went wrong. Instead, you will immediately take a practice swing or two and "feel" the proper swing motions which were missing the moment before.

Swing, Don't Hit

Someone—was it Percy Boomer?—called the hit impulse golf's biggest bogey. My teaching experience indicates that the *hit impulse*—the automatic tendency to strike *at* the ball—is the foremost reason why so few golfers break 80 in their lifetimes. This impulse keeps teaching professionals in business. More than any other golfing habit, this natural tendency is very difficult to reprogram. But to create the effortless swing, our major objective must be to learn to swing the club along an arc with only the most minor regard for the ball. We endeavor, in the words of Ken Venturi, to "swing through the ball, not at it."

In my attempts to help players overcome the dreaded hit impulse, I have seen some students use the keys to hit the ball better with their eyes closed, because then they could not see that round white obstacle in the swing path. Hence, their sequence of motion carried them through the ball to the finish with no disturbing strain or effort before the impact area.

Say Yea (Positive Expectancy)

Anyone who has played golf can recall the disconcerting absence of positive expectancy. The absence manifests itself as an absolute certainty that a lousy shot is about to happen, followed shortly by a statement such as: "I just knew I was going to hit that ball into the lake!"

Deep in the mind, the setup for every shot is accompanied by a loud *yea* or *nay*. The objective, of course, is to believe: "Yes, this is going to be a good shot." Unfortunately, some players stand over the ball while the sun rises and sets and all they ever hear in the mind is "You're going to duff it. You're going to slice it off the course."

If this happens to you, argue with yourself—even lie to yourself if necessary. Remember, a good shot

Say "Si!"—Lee Trevino epitomizes the attitude of positive expectancy.

could happen! When your mind says *nay,* just counter with: "It is possible that I will put this shot in the hole." You will be amazed how much this reduces your tendency to chop at the ball and improves the feel of your swing, as well as its results.

Visualization

Have you ever sat in your car and left the driveway with no destination in mind? Have you ever scheduled a party or a meeting and failed to invite everyone? I surely hope not.

Have you ever hit a golf shot with no exact target in mind? Many people hit shots on the lesson tee without ever looking down the fairway at a target. Others take a cursory, reflexive look, with little or no real focus or attention, as they count down that previously mentioned mental checklist.

We must plan the shot as specifically as possible if our body is to execute our desires. The more exact visual input we provide for our nervous system, the better we can "feel" the upcoming shot. In short, we plan the shot by visualizing it as specifically as possible in our imaginations. I like to "see" the ball blaze down the target line like a comet and explode on an exact landing point. Players who have difficulty visualizing the shot should say aloud exactly what they want the ball to do—a technique used by Lee Trevino—and the picture of the ball flying true to the target will appear immediately.

We keep this image of the target in our minds, in our "second attention," as we enable our bodies to feel the keys which create the effortless swing to the finish.

The Keys to the Effortless Swing

As you may know, there exist many distinct, and often contradictory, methods for hitting golf shots. Some years ago I decided to study as many methods as possible in order to distill out the "common threads," or "methods of the masters." To some extent I was successful, because my search, coupled with considerable teaching experience, allowed me to develop a method which, once and for all, saves students from wandering with hopeful expectation from one set of ideas to the next, overcrowding their minds with an endless sequence of analytical possibilities.

You can use the keys to build a swing which you will keep for life. The sensations of the swing will become familiar and you will learn to trust them. The emphasis, however, is on the word *build*.

The keys are presented in the following chapters in a series of small steps which are easily mastered, but you won't get a new golf swing just by reading about it.

13

Ben Hogan recognized the great value of building muscle memory through practice.

Get up and move your body! The trick is to make each step *muscle memory* before moving on to the succeeding step. Only with this commitment of time and attention firmly in mind can you expect to achieve a lifetime of effortless golf.

There are only five keys to the effortless swing. They are:

1. Balance
2. Momentum

3. Steady swing center
4. Relaxed arms
5. Rhythm

Before we consider each key in detail, let me briefly summarize the elements of the effortless swing.

First, the player establishes and maintains good balance. By virtue of the proper coil, weight shift, and connection, the player creates powerful momentum with the torso, and swings the relaxed, lightweight arms up and down in an arc around the steady swing center to a full finish.

If the sequence of motions is correct, ideal rhythm will be established. That is, the change of direction at the top of the swing will occur slowly, momentum will gradually build, and the fastest moment of the swing will be sensed in the follow-through. The player will finish the swing relaxed and balanced.

We will use the vehicles of the "lighthouse" turn, the basic arc, the three-quarter swing, and the full swing to bring these keys to life in your golf game.

LESSON ONE
Balance

A few teaching professionals assert that the legs are *not* the major source of power in the golf swing. To prove the point, they hit prodigious drives while kneeling on the ground or seated in chairs. For my part, I wonder how far their drives would go if they were hoisted by harness a few inches off the ground. Probably not very far, for even if they do not use their legs, they must use the ground to create force in the swing. The body has to wind up, to coil against the ground. Imagine trying to tee off, wearing slippery shoes, against an icy surface. That would be the ultimate arms-only swing, and it would have a very poor result.

To generate maximum power with a minimum of effort, we employ the entire body, including the large muscles of the legs and back, to swing the club along its arc. These muscles use the ground as a brace against which they coil and uncoil the torso and the shoulders, thus creating the "body turn." So, before discussing

Lower body balance results from a slight inner knee flex, with the golfer's weight slightly to the inside perimeters of the feet. Can you feel a sense of readiness in the legs? The upper body is fairly erect. Tilt the spine forward just enough to let the arms hang freely in front of the body.

in detail the keys to power, we must first establish our relationship with the ground. In other words, we must create good *balance*. Balance is the first key to the effortless swing.

Balance is a feeling, a sensation. Golfers have used many images to illustrate the sensation of good balance in the setup. Feel like a cat ready to spring. Feel as though you were about to jump straight up in the air. Feel as though you were about to catch a heavy bag of cement. Feel as though you could withstand a heavy wind from any direction. Feel as if you were entering the ring with a sumo wrestler.

The Knees

Begin with a slight flex to the knees. I see no need to lock either knee joint at any time during the swing. To do so would sacrifice balance. On the other hand, excess knee flex makes the legs feel sluggish during the swing. So let's say *slight knee flex*.

Should the knees flex inward, outward, toward the hole, or straight ahead? Certainly there exists here a variety of opinion among experts. I strongly recommend a slight *inward* knee flex, as if one were holding a volleyball between the knees, or there existed a magnetic attraction pulling the knees toward each other.

This will tend to put the body weight on the inside edges of the feet—you feel as if you have fallen arches. Some teachers advocate putting the weight on the heels. I challenge them to name another sport where one puts the weight on the heels. In many cases, having the weight on the heels leads players to counterbalance their rear ends (which will tend to stick out) with their heads. The result is too much bend at the waist, which inhibits leg and hip action, causing additional weight-shift and balance problems.

So, lower-body balance calls for a *slight* inner knee flex with the weight *slightly* to the inside edges of the feet. You should be able to bounce slightly with a sense of readiness in the legs. Can you feel it?

The Upper Body

The position of the upper body is simple. Do not cave in the chest and curve the spine. Stretch the spine up, feeling the chest expand somewhat. Tilt the spine forward slightly to enable the arms to hang loosely in front of the thighs. The spine tilt gives the arms enough room to swing freely.

You may feel as if you are about to sit on a high bar stool. The head is held *up*. The upper body is relaxed, lightweight. The primary sensations are the inward knee flex and the feeling of standing tall, re-laxed, and ready. Again, the arms hang loosely in front of the body.

Each key is built upon the one before it, so please establish this sensation as a *reflexive position* you assume without much thought. Anticipate the feel of it, then *do* it. It may take a few days, or a week, or a month. Practice it at home, at work, in line at the bank. On the golf course, maintain the balance from the setup, throughout the swing, to the finish position. We will

discuss this in more detail, but, for now, take what-
ever time you need to stand and get set up with good
balance, and then proceed to the second key to the
effortless swing.

LESSON TWO
Momentum

Everyone agrees that the major factor influencing distance in a golf shot is clubhead speed. An important priority, then, is to create enough *momentum* to accelerate the club through the impact zone to the finish of the swing. We accomplish this with three related ingredients: coil, weight shift, and connection.

Proper use of coil, weight shift, and connection will help us overcome the hit impulse, which creates momentum primarily through the arms, and especially the right arm, throwing the club at the ball. Instead, we will use the body to throw our almost weightless arms through the downswing into the follow-through arc. We will use the *torso* to generate arm and shaft speed.

Since this concept is really the heart of the effortless swing, let me offer some examples.

Occasionally, I will ask one of my students to throw a golf club as far as he or she can, using only the arms. The results are not impressive. Next, I ask the student to throw it using the legs (a natural weight shift then occurs) and the hips and torso to help the fling. Naturally, the club moves faster and flies farther. Try the same test by throwing a golf ball, or a Frisbee. The point becomes quite obvious in those contexts, yet the golfer must be trained how to use the legs and torso to swing the arms and launch the ball.

The Coil

The first element of momentum—our second key—is *coil* or body turn. I frequently refer to the backswing as the *windup*. The hips and shoulders turn around the spine, away from the target. Essentially, the back is turned to the target and the chest faces away from the target. While the shoulders complete this 90-degree turn, the hips turn also, but only about half as much, say 45 degrees. The spine stays exactly where it was at address, simply twisting in place.

Because of the inward knee pressure established earlier, the *left knee* goes with the turn and *flexes in toward the right,* pointing behind the ball. The inward knee pressure should hold the right knee more or less in place, flexed above the instep of the right foot. The player should feel considerable pressure on the right knee in the coiled position. If the right knee sways or straightens up and locks, the swing is likely to fail. In fact, many players will benefit by actually *bending the right knee a little more* as they windup (as Jack Nicklaus does).

A good checkpoint for building the coil is to *wind up the left shoulder until it reaches a point just above the right knee and hip*. The golfer will feel, again, pressure on the inside of the flexed right leg, plus a stretched sensation in the left side of the torso.

Try this move in front of a full-length mirror, pointing your arms straight out in front of you, at the mirror, as you establish your balanced position. In order to move the left shoulder around to a point above the right hip, you will need to make a *fairly level shoulder turn,* not a big downward dip of the left shoulder.

You may also notice a very slight tilt of the spine away from the target. A slight tilt to the right is far preferable to any tilt whatsoever to the left, which could cause almost anything but a good shot. Of course, it is perfectly fine to keep the spine where it was at address, with no tilt to the right. The turn then will be a few degrees smaller, but the coiling sensation will still result. In either case, the shoulder, hip, and knee movements will feel quite level.

The Lighthouse Turn

Because the coiling motion does not directly involve the use of the arms, I wish to discuss arm action in the swing later on. For the present, extend your arms directly out in front of you at chest height, placing your palms together. Now your arms and shoulders form a *triangle,* which, for the time being, will turn in an arc, *parallel to the ground,* at shoulder height, as the body coils.

The arms should feel relaxed, almost weightless, as if you were holding a slice of bread between your palms. As we continue this discussion of coil, weight

Coil position (side view). The triangle made by the arms and shoulders remains intact as the player coils the torso against the brace of the right leg.

shift, and connection, there will be no additional muscle activity in the arms. The relaxed triangle you are forming will glide in an arc with the coiling motion of the shoulders and torso. I call this the lighthouse turn, because the turning triangle reminds me of the sweeping arc of the bright beam from a lighthouse.

Summarizing our discussion of the coil, windup, or body turn, let's emphasize two primary sensations. *First,* the left shoulder turns to a point above the right knee and hip, causing a stretching sensation in the left side. *Second,* the right knee is flexed slightly inward, giving the sensations of pressure on the knee and body weight on the inside of the right foot. The completed shoulder turn is largely responsible for putting the weight on the inside of the right foot. The right knee and foot position create a brace, or pivot point, for the coil. The golfer should feel wound up, ready to spring back in the other direction. *Please read this paragraph several times.* These positions and sensations are vital components of the swing.

To assure that you have coiled properly, consider these secondary checkpoints.

The relaxed arm and shoulder triangle has turned about 90 degrees to the right, pointing roughly 180 degrees away from the target. The left foot has rolled to the right because the knee flexed inward. The left heel his risen an inch or two from the ground. The head has remained steady, facing straight ahead.

Of course, the purpose of the windup is to enable us to uncoil and deliver an acceleration of arm and club-shaft speed through the downswing into the follow-through.

The Weight Shift

The manner in which the uncoiling motion is initiated separates the good players from the hackers. I cannot emphasize that statement too strongly. To uncoil properly, the player must begin the "change of direction" by *shifting the body weight*. In essence, the uncoiling motion, which swings the arms and creates shaft speed, must begin at the ground and work up the body. Most bad players totally abuse this swing fundamental. Instead, they yank on the club with their arms, totally wasting the energy stored in the coil.

To uncoil in a powerful motion, the player shifts the body weight from the right pivot point to the left foot, thus creating a *left pivot point* which will support the uncoiling and downswing. This is accomplished by pushing off the right foot—by *pushing the right knee toward the ball*. As the uncoiling motion continues, the right knee will continue moving until it touches the left knee.

Observe the position of the knees on any good player at the finish of the swing. Invariably, the knees touch or almost touch each other. Poor players, on the other hand, often finish their swings with their knees spread quite far apart.

Here's a useful image that will remind you to move your knees properly as you uncoil. Imagine you have a pair of cymbals (like the ones used in marching bands) attached to the insides of your knees, one cymbal on each knee. As you begin the change of direction by shifting your weight, *clash* the cymbal on your right knee into the cymbal on your left knee. The uncoiling motion will feel smooth and effortless.

I do *not* wish to imply that either the right knee or the left knee initiates the change of direction by moving *toward the target*. I take exception to this notion for these reasons:

By first moving the *right* knee toward the target instead of toward the ball, the player tends to shift the weight to the left heel, thus weakening the left pivot point. This often results in an outside-in arc with a very flat follow-through, causing pulls, pull-hooks, and slices.

By first driving the *left* knee toward the target, the player often sways laterally to the left, moving the left knee and body weight to the outside of the left foot, thus destroying the left pivot point. The frequently disappointing results include loss of balance and moving the swing center, which creates thin shots, as well as pushed and sliced shots.

Ideally, the player establishes stability and balance on the left pivot point by shifting *the right knee toward the ball* to begin the uncoiling motion. The left knee, which was flexed inward, pointing behind the ball, will move, in tandem with the movement of the right knee, to a point just above the left foot. As a result of these knee movements, *the left heel will return to the ground and the body weight will first be planted on the inside of the left foot*. By planting the body weight firmly on the left foot, the player establishes the left pivot point, which braces the body during the downswing.

Of course, the weight may shift to the outside of the left foot as the swing nears completion; but I strongly advocate that the majority of the body weight be planted firmly on the left foot as the clubhead strikes the ball. The resulting feeling of solid contact will be a first for many players. I often tell my students: "If you cannot feel the weight shift solidly to the left foot, don't bother to swing down, because you will not appreciate the result!" The great Jack Nicklaus advocates the feeling of keeping the weight on the *inside* of the left foot during the downswing and through impact with the ball.

Let us briefly recap our discussion thus far. You first establish good balance, primarily by means of a slight inward knee flex. Your arms are extended comfortably directly out in front of your body. Palms touch lightly, forming a triangle with the shoulders. You coil the torso by turning the left shoulder until it is in line with your inwardly flexed right knee. Your weight feels solidly on the inside perimeter of the right foot. You then initiate the uncoiling motion by shifting the body weight to the *entire inside* of the left foot. This is easily accomplished by driving the right knee toward the ball.

If you are with me this far, you will notice that the uncoiling motion of the hips and shoulders has already begun. As the right knee moves and the body weight shifts, the belt buckle turns a few degrees toward the target. It feels virtually effortless to continue this uncoiling motion of the hips until the belt buckle faces the target and your knees touch.

The Hips or the Knees?

The uncoiling motion of the hips produces a very pleasant sensation of power and freedom. I believe the rotation of the hips is a major source of momentum.

THE LIGHTHOUSE TURN (front view). The triangle glides in an arc like a lighthouse beam as the player creates effortless momentum.

1. *The starting position.*
2. *The coil position. Turn the left shoulder to a point above the flexed right leg. Feel the stored-up power in the coil.*
3. Initiate the uncoiling motion *by moving the right knee towards the ball. This automatically shifts the weight to the inside of the left foot. The hips unwind, continuing the uncoiling motion, pulling the arms around towards the target.*
4. *Finish position for the lighthouse turn. The torso faces the target; the triangle remains intact. The body weight is solid on the left foot. The right foot is straight up and down. The belly arches slightly towards the target.*
5. *Imagine cymbals attached to your knees. Clash them together (as you unwind) to feel your knees control the uncoiling motion.*

Occasionally, on the lesson tee, I abandon all discussion of the knees, and even the weight shift, and focus instead on "hip action" to help a frustrated player create momentum. It usually works.

Basically, I suggest unwinding the belt buckle or belly or lower torso and arching it *slightly* toward the target. The hip turn, again, feels quite level during the windup and uncoiling, but it may rise *slightly* just after the belt buckle passes through the ball and arch *slightly* toward the target. I emphasize "slightly" because if the hips rise too soon or too much, the player "comes off the ball" and the shot is ruined.

I have no great argument with any teacher who says: Throw your belly (or fanny) toward the target." I just prefer, in most cases, to build a specific, repeatable weight shift using proper knee action, because I believe good knee work contributes to good balance, keeps the swing center steady, and thereby builds consistency—something none of us can get enough of. Too much emphasis on hip action, at the expense of the knees and weight shift, tends to endanger balance and may create a big lateral sway to the left on the downswing. This moves the swing center and shifts the weight too far to the outside of the left foot, which often causes the player to rock back and finish the swing on the right foot, completely confused about what has happened.

As a side note, some more advanced players combat that tendency by keeping their right heels planted on the ground through impact while making that powerful hip turn. This keeps them very steady over the ball, but I consider it an advanced technique which should be tried only by a player who already has a repeatable weight shift built into his or her swing.

In the meantime, let's build a strong coil with a reliable weight shift (controlled by the knees) and then enjoy the response of smooth, powerful hip and torso motion.

More Lighthouse Turn

What happens to the arm and shoulder triangle while the lower body uncoils?

You should find that the triangle is pulled or dragged smoothly around until it points either at the target or slightly to the left of it. The triangle should glide effortlessly around, in an arc parallel to the ground, creating the lighthouse turn (picture the sweeping arc of a lighthouse beam).

How this horizontal arc five feet above the ball position applies to a golf swing will become clear when we progress to a discussion of arm action in the swing. Right now, there is *no* arm action, only the gliding motion of the triangle.

Connection

In order to clarify how the uncoiling of the hips serves to turn the shoulders and arms, I must refer to a term introduced by Jimmy Ballard in his excellent book *How to Perfect Your Golf Swing*. Ballard asserts that all great athletes exhibit *connection,* or a "natural sequential wholeness" of body motion. I use the term in discussing three aspects of the creation of momentum.

1.   The inward knee pressure invisibly connects the knees, enabling them to work in unison to create balance, power, and consistency.
2.   The arms and shoulders (as discussed so far) connect in a triangle *which does not change shape* as it moves in an arc with the coiling motion.
3.   Most important, the muscles on the sides of the body (the latissimus dorsi) and the abdominal muscles firm up enough to connect the hips to the shoulders, ensuring that they move in unison throughout the coiling and uncoiling.

This all-important *connection between the hips and shoulders* is totally absent in two common and ineffective forms of downswing. The first, and by far the more frequent, results from the hit impulse. The golfer starts the downswing (there's no guarantee he ever actually "coiled") by yanking on the club with the arms and throwing the right shoulder down and around. In such cases, the hips turn, if at all, well after the ball is hit—or mishit!

In the second case, the player concentrates on initiating the uncoiling motion with the knees and hips, and does a fine job. Unfortunately, the latissimus dorsi and abdominal muscles stretch with the movement, leaving the shoulders motionless as the hips uncoil. When this happens, the momentum created by the weight shift and hip turn fails to influence the shoulders, and the golfer has no choice but to attack with the arms. Such a swing feels very disjointed and unpleasant, and not at all effortless.

A modification of this error occurs in the lighthouse turn when the player correctly feels the hips unwind the shoulders, but mistakenly allows the triangle to break down, and lets the left arm collapse against the chest. Thus the momentum of the uncoiling motion moves the hips and shoulders, but not the arms, so the golfer is again forced to unload with the right arm.

So, I emphasize that to establish our second key, momentum, we need *connection,* especially between the hips and shoulders, to guarantee an effective coil and weight shift.

A major reason I present "momentum" in the context of a horizontal arc of the triangle (lighthouse turn) is to help the player feel the *function* of connection. As the player shifts the weight and rotates the hips, the triangle retains its shape and immediately is pulled in an arc and gains momentum as it passes the ball.

It is acceptable to assert that in the uncoiling, as soon as the belt buckle moves, so do the fingertips. In Ben Hogan's *Five Lessons,* the great master introduces a helpful image of connection. At the top of the backswing, he extends a cord from his belt buckle to his left wrist. When the belt buckle turns on the downswing, the cord pulls the arms and shoulders in unison, creating a connected uncoiling motion. I believe Byron Nelson also employs a swing key which illustrates this feeling of connection. He likes to feel his lower left side and back pull the club on the downswing. As you must agree, that feeling is a far cry from the familiar feeling in the right arm and shoulder when giving in to the hit impulse.

We are now making considerable progress. You are balanced, and are creating plenty of momentum thanks to the coil, weight shift, and connection. But we still have not swung a club or hit a ball. To do so properly requires building proper arm action. But first I would like to "polish up" the material presented thus far, and add a few observations about the finish position of the lighthouse turn to present our third key, a steady swing center.

LESSON THREE
A Steady Swing Center

The Key to a Consistent Arc

Using coil, weight shift, and connection to create powerful momentum will prove profitable only if we can guarantee that the swing motion moves in a predictable, repeatable arc through space. No one wants to hit the ball 250 yards off the golf course! Because the golf ball is so small, and the target is so far away, and the margins for error are so unforgiving, we have no chance against Old Man Par unless we build a consistent swing arc.

The most important requirement to this end is maintaining a steady swing center—a fixed hub of the swing arc. The prolific Jack Nicklaus, in *Golf My Way* and all his other writings, asserts that a steady head is the one universal golf fundamental. Since the head has such a range of motion relative to the spine, I prefer to refer to the *top of the spine* as the swing center or hub. If the head is steady, the swing center will be,

37

A steady swing center is the one universal golf fundamental. Visualize the top of your spine as your swing center.

too. If the head swivels slightly or cocks slightly to the right or left during the swing, it is still possible to maintain a steady swing center at the top of the spine.

So my goal for you now is to create momentum in the lighthouse turn while keeping the top of your spine approximately perpendicular to the target line. Your shoulders and torso will wind and unwind around a fixed point. As I mentioned earlier, a slight tilt of the spine away from the target on the backswing is acceptable to build a more powerful coil; in the uncoiling motion, your spine can return to its perpendicular position before the clubhead meets the ball. On the other hand, tilting the spine toward the target on the backswing guarantees disaster.

Try the lighthouse turn in front of a mirror. Sight on something in the background behind your head to indicate whether your swing center moves from right to left or up and down during the motion. If you have followed directions to this point, I doubt your head is bobbing up and down, because you have built a strong coil (or rotary) motion into your swing, and the turn of your triangle is parallel to the ground throughout. Neither is it likely that your head is finishing to the right of its initial position. If it is, you either are failing to shift your weight from your right foot, or are shifting to the outside of your left foot, causing you to fall back in a big "reverse C" position, ending up with considerable weight on the right foot again.

If anything, your swing center tilts to the left, toward the target, when you finish uncoiling. The power of the motion pulls your whole upper body toward the target, and your head moves closer to the target than any part of your torso.

Keeping It Steady

I am not going to proffer a lengthy discourse on how a moving swing center destroys golf shots. Other instruction books, notably Nicklaus's *Golf My Way,* have demonstrated these problems. (I know there are pictures in existence showing how the heads of good players move down and back at impact, but do you think those players are *trying* to move their heads down and back?) Instead, I wish to offer a few simple techniques to help build a steady swing center.

First, relax the triangle, while still maintaining its shape. Any abrupt muscle activity in the upper arms and shoulders will cause a jerkiness which will destroy the natural flow we are creating and could jostle your swing center.

Second, finish the lighthouse turn with your knees touching and your belt buckle two or three inches closer to the target than your face. Check yourself in the mirror or go outside and check using your shadow. This should feel very pleasant, and is the major sensation or position which guarantees the success of our third key—the steady swing center.

Another suggestion to help you maintain a steady swing center while hitting golf shots is to watch the ball disappear. Focusing the eyes on a specific spot surely helps create steadiness, and I prefer watching the ball disappear to watching the clubhead hit the ball because I do not want you to think about *hitting* the ball.

Another good tip is to learn to "stay behind the ball" during the downswing. Once you have established repeatable balance and momentum, you can more reliably achieve the proper finish position by becoming aware of staying behind the ball with your upper body.

If all else fails, it is sometimes helpful to feel as if the shoulders turn exactly in place throughout the swing. However, while these suggestions and others are usually helpful, the most reliable way to achieve a steady swing center is to *build knee action* which shifts the weight to the *insides* of the feet and creates stable pivot points.

I cannot emphasize strongly enough the importance of building this lighthouse turn as a repeatable, enjoyable reflexive motion. I emphasize doing it thousands of times without a golf club or ball, *to build the muscle memory* of a correct sequence of body motions. Do it, again, in front of a mirror, or outside in the daylight when you can observe your shadow to monitor your steady swing center. You will be piling pebbles on the "scales of swing tendency" to offset the muscle memory of the countless hit impulses your body has produced.

The elements of the finish position of the lighthouse turn serve as checkpoints to ensure that you build the ideal muscle memory:

▶ In the finish position, the weight is *very* solid on the left foot. It is acceptable when *slightly* to the outside of the foot, but not when completely to the outside of the left heel.

▶ The left leg is *slightly* flexed. The left knee is over the left foot. The right knee touches the left knee (or very nearly). The right foot is directly perpendicular to the ground.

▶ The belt buckle faces the target, a few inches closer to the target than your face. The relaxed arm-shoulder triangle points to the target or slightly to the left of it. It was pulled to this finish position by virtue of a connected body motion controlled by balance, coil, and weight shift.

Now, put this book down and practice this light-house turn five or ten minutes or more each day for a week or two, until you can do it without thinking about anything but how nice it feels. After a thousand or more repetitions, you will be 75 percent of the way to a powerful, effortless, and repeatable swing.

Lesson Four
Relaxed Arms

If you are with me so far, you probably feel highly confident regarding your ability to rebuild your swing with the emphasis on effortlessness. By now you have a vivid sensation of the true source of power in the swing. The legs, the torso, and the body weight combine to accelerate the arms and club shaft along the desired arc around a fixed swing center.

To transform our lighthouse turn into a true golf swing, we now add the element of proper arm action.

As you grip the club directly out in front of the body, the arm-shoulder triangle might be accurately described as a lowercase letter **y**. The left arm and club shaft form the straight-line side of the **y**, while the right arm approaches the left arm and club shaft at an angle.

As you look into a mirror, the line from the left shoulder through the left arm and club shaft to the ball should be straight. With the club extended straight ahead in the lighthouse-turn position, the leading edge of the clubface will be straight up and down, perpendicular to the ground.

A Few Words on the Grip

Forgive me if I do not present a lengthy discourse on the nuances of the proper golf grip. Many teachers before me have done an admirable job, most notably Ben Hogan in his *Five Lessons*. Thus my recommendations will be few.

The palms should face each other. The back of the left hand and the palm of the right should align to the target, as if the clubhead were glued onto the back of the left hand. The club is wedged under the heel pad of the left hand and lies across the left palm to the first knuckle of the left index finger.

The right-hand grip is established primarily in the two middle fingers, definitely not in the palm. The **v** or line formed between the thumb and index fingers of each hand points between the player's chin and right shoulder. The thumb of each hand lies slightly to the opposite side of the shaft.

On the subject of grip pressure, I do not wish to take an adamant stand. Some golfers play well with a firm grip, others with an extremely light grip. I do advocate maintaining a *constant* grip pressure as much as possible, because many potentially sound swings are ruined by a sudden tightening of grip pressure sometime before impact. So, if you choose a light grip pressure, be sure your fingers do not loosen on the club

*The lighthouse turn with a club. The **y** made by the arms and club glides smoothly in a horizontal arc as the torso creates effortless momentum.*

during the swing. Conversely, if you prefer a firmer grip pressure, do not allow muscle tension to creep into your wrist joints, arms, or shoulders. Tensed wrists, arms, and shoulders guarantee disappointing shots.

Relaxed, limber arms and shoulders help create a free, fast, smooth arm and club swing to a full finish.

In fact, our fourth key to the effortless swing is to *develop relaxed arm movements throughout the swing*. The momentum created by coil, weight shift, and connection will produce greater and more effortless distance and accuracy when the arms remain relatively free from tension. That is *the* secret.

You should now compare the swing sensations resulting from maintaining a relaxed upper body against those experienced when the upper body becomes stiff and rigid. Try this while swinging the club along a lighthouse-turn arc, keeping the triangle (or **y**) intact. The first swing should be done, as before, with relaxed and limber arms. The fact that we added a club to our horizontal swing arc should not affect the swing sensations; the club is merely an extension of the relaxed, extended left arm. The arms and club will be pulled around by the uncoiling motion. The motion feels fluid and effortless.

Before starting the second swing, tense the entire upper body—arms, hands, shoulders, chest, and back. Creating a lighthouse-turn arc now will be quite a strain. You might also move your swing center and may even lose your balance. A similar swing sensation (one you recognize?) can be experienced by coiling for the lighthouse turn with a relaxed triangle, then, as the uncoiling is about to commence, abruptly stiffening the upper body muscles. The resulting unpleasant sensations probably include a deceleration of the club shaft, disconnection, loss of balance, and unnecessary strain.

The Key to the Keys

I used to term the relaxed arm swing "the free arm swing," because the arms fly freely through the ball position to the finish of the swing without the interruption of tension or of sudden deliberate force applied in the impact zone. However, the term "free" proved misleading, because the relaxed arms are not "free." They are essentially passive, and are subservient to the torso motions which create momentum. In short, the essential precept of the effortless swing is that *the arms do not swing the club: The body swings the arms and the club* to a full finish.

Using the body to swing the arms increases both the distance and the accuracy of our golf shots. Greater distance results because the larger muscles of the legs, back, and torso create greater momentum, enabling the lightweight arms and the club to accelerate along the arc at greater speeds. Moreover, the buildup of speed will not peak too soon, as it often does when only the arms swing the club, causing a deceleration of the club as it nears impact with the ball.

Greater accuracy results because the swing arc created when the body coils around the swing center is highly repeatable. If the arms perform in a connected, subservient manner relative to that coiling motion, the resulting arm-and-club-shaft arc will be highly consistent. Consistency is the bedrock in developing accuracy.

The arms have the greatest range of motion of all the parts of the body. Therefore, we cannot expect the arms to create a consistent, repeatable swing arc on an exact line at the correct angle through that tiny golf ball unless we restrict their movements to those controlled by the coiling of the torso around a fixed point.

Moreover, if we mistakenly create the swing arc primarily with the arms, we have no guarantee that the torso will coil or uncoil. We can trust our coiling motion to swing the arms, but we cannot expect an arm swing to coil the torso.

To experience such a limited "free arm swing," assume the stance for the lighthouse turn and swing the club around the body with the arms while keeping the hips and shoulders motionless, facing forward. Feels ridiculous? In this context, it certainly does. Yet many players swing in *exactly* this manner: They swing the club across their relatively stationary bodies with their arms. No doubt you have witnessed—or even experienced—the results: topped and fat and smothered shots, slices, pulled hooks, and outright misses.

The Arms Move Up and Down

This may come as a surprise, but, for the most part, the arms do not move the club across the body during the swing. Instead, *the arms move the club up and down in front of the body* as it winds up and unwinds. To illustrate this we will add the first portion of arm movement to our lighthouse-turn arc and create a different swing, which I call *the basic arc*. Fortunately, you have already learned most of the movements used to create the basic arc.

Isolate the arm movements in the basic arc by moving the **y** directly up and down in a line in front of the body from the ground to waist high. Note that the arm movement originates in the shoulder joint. The upper body does not change position.

The new arm movement adds a vertical, or up-and-down, element to the lighthouse turn. To this point in our swing-building process, we have been unable to hit a ball unless we place it on a tee four or five feet high. To make contact with a ball on the ground, we obviously need to lower the club.

Assume the stance for the lighthouse turn, club and arms extended directly out in front of the chest. (Remember, the knees are flexed inward slightly, and the spine is tilted just slightly forward toward the ball.) Now, first lower the **y** made by the arms and club shaft to about waist height. This is the "top" of the basic arc. There should be no movement in the back or torso as you continue to lower the **y** until the clubhead nearly touches the ground. For now, this is the bottom of the basic arc.

We can isolate the arm movements (relative to the torso) in the basic arc by moving the **y** directly up and down in front of the body, so that the clubhead moves up and down in a line in front of the body from the ground to waist height.

Notice that this arm movement originates from the shoulder joint only. The elbows and wrists have not influenced the movement, and the **y** has retained its shape as it moves up and down. (I am being extremely explicit here because I cannot work with you in person, so I must try to anticipate possible incorrect movements or misinterpretations.)

Now you can assume your stance with the **y** at the "bottom" of the basic arc, lightly touching the ground. (The bottom of the downswing arc will be slightly lower, but let's leave that for later.) The imaginary ball should be positioned to the left of center of your stance, say off your left ear. The butt end of the club will be directly above the ball, slightly closer to the target than the clubhead, on a line pointing to the left shoulder.

Creating the Basic Arc

Your task now is to coil the torso just as before: left shoulder coiling to the right hip, right knee flexing inward and forming the pivot point on the inside of the right foot. Now, however, you simply move the **y** up to waist height as your body turns. The club is still in front of your body, which has turned 90 degrees away from the target. You have completed the backswing of the basic arc.

Questions will surely arise concerning the timing of the upward motion of the **y** as the body coils on the backswing. Actually, you could complete either motion before starting the other one. For example, you could raise the **y** and then coil; or coil, then raise the **y**. I suggest initiating the coiling motion first, to move the clubhead back just above the ground for a foot or so (until the coil starts to turn the clubhead in from the target line), and then raise the **y** to the waist-height position. I recommend this because it feels most comfortable, and also because it helps assure that the player coils the body. Lifting the arms and club too soon tends to inhibit the coiling motion and creates an arm-dominant action which swings the club outside the target line.

THE BASIC ARC

1. *The setup position.*
2. *The coil position (side view). Note the similarity to the coil position of the lighthouse turn. The* **y** *has retained its shape. It is relaxed and ready to drop down.*
3. *Impact! The shifting of the weight and uncoiling of the torso was well-timed with the dropping of the* **y**.
4. *The momentum (created by the torso motion) swings the relaxed arms to the follow-through position. Note the similarity to the finish of the lighthouse turn.*

The major checkpoints for the backswing of the basic arc are virtually the same as those for the windup in the lighthouse turn. Of course, it is essential to achieve the coiled sensation created by the shoulder turn and the body weight on the right pivot point. The relaxed **y** will extend directly out from the body, waist-high, at about 180 degrees from the target. *The leading edge of the clubface should be straight up and down, or perpendicular to the ground.*

Now the moment of truth is upon us. We have gone to considerable effort to overcome the hit impulse on the downswing, so we will initiate the downswing (notice the term *down*) by shifting the weight and un-coiling the torso, not by hitting with the arms. *As the body begins to unwind,* creating momentum, the **y** formed by the arms and club will merely fall, or drop down, to the bottom of its arc and sweep through the ball position until the uncoiling motion pulls it up again to point at the target, at waist or chest height.

I must emphasize that the arms *do not* push or pull the club across the body, or down, or anywhere else. As the weight shift leads the uncoiling motion, the relaxed **y** automatically will drop down. Gravity will be helping.

Which Comes First?

Some teachers contend that the club drops down before the weight shift initiates the downswing. I believe this approach often causes the player to hit the ground behind the ball, ruining the shot. On the other hand, lowering the **y** too late causes the player to swing "outside in" across the target line, also ruining the shot. Admittedly, this is a tricky situation.

Ideally, the motions are virtually simultaneous. (Different players may need to feel as if one or the other move happens slightly earlier, so experiment with it.) The knees shift the weight and the relaxed **y** drops down as it is pulled around. *Don't be afraid to let the* **y** *drop straight down,* as if it were going to hit the outside of your right foot. You may say: "It feels like I didn't do anything, but it felt good." If so, you have made me very happy, because you are having your first sampling of the effortless swing.

It is important to realize that the shoulders begin to unwind just *after* the arms begin to drop. This is because the unwinding motion works up the body, and *the shoulders must wait for the hip turn* to begin and (via connection) to start to pull the shoulders around.

Please review the finish positions for the lighthouse turn discussed in Lesson Two. To these you will need to add only one checkpoint for the basic arc. The **y** made by the arms and club shaft will point to the target and the leading edge of the clubface will be perpendicular to the ground. Once again the arms remain relaxed, almost weightless. And, of course, the swing center is steady.

Where Is the Bottom of the Arc?

Try the above swing a number of times with no ball. You should expect to "clip" the ground to the left of the ball position, out near your left foot. The shifting of the body weight to the left serves to lower the bottom of the arc and move it slightly to the left, more toward the target.

As we begin to hit balls with the basic arc, we will be striking the ball on the downward arc. The

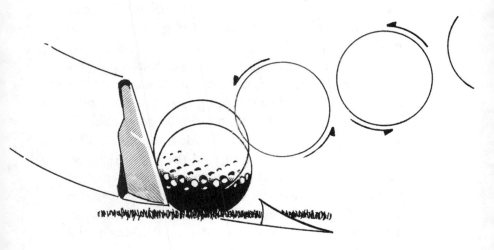

The clubhead strikes the ball just before *it reaches the bottom of its arc. After impact, the ball rises as the clubhead continues* down *into the turf.*

clubface and the ball will meet, then backspin will cause the ball to rise while the clubhead continues down into the ground before rising again to the completion of the arc. Thus, *the ball and the clubhead will not rise together.*

I mention this because many players will use the hands and arms to try to swing the club *up* at impact, hoping thereby to lift the ball. The result is usually a "ground ball" or "worm-burner" caused by swinging the leading edge of the clubhead up into the ball and imparting topspin to it. So I suggest letting (not *making*) the **y** swing down through the ball as the body turns. The momentum will swing the **y** up again at the proper time, *if the arms are relaxed*. In fact, if we have built the correct sequence of moves, it is virtually impossible to keep the **y** from swinging up to the finish position.

One more caution is necessary, because players frequently interfere with the swing motions of the basic arc by intensely tightening their grip pressure and pulling up with their shoulders during the downswing in fearful anticipation of impact with the ground. This will certainly ruin the swing and the shot. Any necessary change in grip pressure during the downswing will occur automatically and should be imperceptible to the player. Therefore, I suggest you endeavor to keep a constant grip pressure during the swing, and especially on the downswing.

I hope you can now confidently create a basic arc (also called the one-lever swing), feeling your legs and torso swing your arms and club effortlessly along a semicircular upward-downward arc. The ball position is merely one point along the arc, *and you are making no sudden adjustments or effort to influence it.*

If you have mastered this, we are ready to create golf shots.

Even if you are an experienced player, place the ball on a tee initially when you hit shots with the basic arc. Teeing it up reduces any tendency to flinch from fear of hitting the ground.

Hitting Shots

Start with a 7-iron, or any iron between the pitching wedge and the 5-iron. Always use a tee initially, to increase your chances of success. Even if you are an experienced player, try this first with a tee to help reduce any tendency to flinch from hitting the ground.

Now, place the ball just left of center in your stance, in line with your left ear (our ball position for the basic arc). Now use the body to swing the **y** back and up, then down and through. Your keys—balance, momentum, steady center, and relaxed arms—are more than a match for the hit impulse if you have properly committed them to muscle memory.

You can watch the ball disappear off the tee, or you can close your eyes and still make a fine shot. The ball will fly off the tee, say ten to fifty yards, and you will feel a sense of freedom and effortlessness. It is hard to believe, when you first feel it, how little effort is involved and how lightly the ball impedes the arc of the clubhead. This is the feeling that probably gave rise to the saying: "Let the clubhead do the work."

If you are unsuccessful in your attempt to make a golf shot and produce this feeling with the basic arc, fear not. Before we hit any more balls, and certainly before we expand the arc by adding arm and wrist action, we must discuss our final swing key, the very essence of the effortless swing: the feeling of good rhythm.

LESSON FIVE
Rhythm

As our final weapon in the war we wage against the hit impulse, good swing rhythm is our *coup de grace*.

For our purposes, swing rhythm is defined as the changing rates of speed at which the club travels during the swing. The club changes speed almost continually as it moves along its arc. It moves relatively faster through some points along the arc, and relatively slower through other points. Our goal is to use our swing keys to move the club at the optimal speeds at the proper points along the arc.

In his enlightening book *Tempo,* Al Geiberger observes that we have only one fast moment in each swing. In other words, our swing speed *peaks* at a certain point along the arc. Of course, we want that peak speed to occur as the clubhead swings into the ball. Most players rarely achieve peak speed at impact, however, because the hit impulse causes them to waste most of their speed early in the downswing. During your practice sessions, observe your swing to determine where your fastest moment occurs.

In my opinion, the player's sensation of where in the swing the "fast moment" occurs is usually inaccurate. The player senses the fast moment *after* it happens, and feels as if it occurred at a point slightly farther along the arc than where it actually did peak. Therefore, when a swing achieves peak speed during impact with the ball, the player will experience the fastest moment in the *follow-through* after impact. This, in fact, is the major sensory element of the effortless swing.

So, let me repeat myself. During a successful effortless swing, the "fastest moment" is *experienced* in the follow-through. Of course, the clubhead will actually slow down in the follow-through because of impact with the ball, but it will not feel that way to the player. This is as it should be, because impact with the ball lasts only about a two-thousandth of a second. Certainly we cannot expect to "time" the swing to such a minute instant.

Most average-to-poor players make the mistake of trying to apply speed directly to the clubhead as the downswing begins. This does not work very well—as you will probably have discovered! It sometimes helps to picture the ideal force as a small weight that "spins" off the body as it unwinds, travels through the arms, and slides down the shaft into the clubhead at or beyond impact.

This imaginary weight, which represents the transfer of centrifugal force, will actually enable the speed of the club shaft to *pull the arms into the follow-through position*. This feeling gives rise to my suggestion

Gene Littler is well-known for his flawless swing rhythm.

that your swing should feel as if you were going to let the club fly *out of your hands to the target* on the follow-through.

I used to tell players, "Save the speed for the follow-through." This image worked well for some and poorly for others, who would mistakenly fight the natural buildup of momentum caused by the keys. They would fear swinging too fast, and thus tighten the upper body and "quit" on the shot. Needless to say, they would have difficulty identifying *any* fast moment in the swing. So I choose my words carefully and advise you to *let the momentum build* slowly and gradually until the fastest moment is *felt* in the follow-through.

For the many lifetime victims of the hit impulse, this is a foreign feeling. Yet, if you have utilized our keys of balance, momentum, steady center, and relaxed arms, the fastest moment in the basic arc will seem to occur in the follow-through. If it occurs before impact, you are no doubt *pushing* the triangle with your upper body instead of *pulling* it with your legs and torso.

The Changing Speeds

While the main element of good swing rhythm is the feeling of peak speed in the follow-through, the relative club-shaft speeds during the earlier stages of the swing are also vitally important. These other areas to consider are the speed at the start of the backswing, the finish of the backswing, the start of the downswing, and the area just before impact with the ball. Let's discuss them in sequential order.

There are some good players who make fast initial backswings, or takeaways, but there are a lot more bad players who "start it back" fast. The initiation of the backswing will feel quite fast when the arms and hands "snatch" the club away from the ball. When the player instead makes a connected "one-piece" coiling motion of the body and triangle to move the club away from the ball, the takeaway feels slower. So the speed of the takeaway is important only as an indicator of what parts of the body are moving the club. For that reason, I prefer the terms "windup" and "coil" to the term "backswing." In any event, as I'm sure you will agree, there are no prizes awarded for a fast backswing!

Neither do we want the club to accelerate dramatically as the backswing nears completion. When the club accelerates near the top of the backswing, we can be sure the arms have taken over control of the swing and will ruin the shot via the hit impulse. I have seen a great number of potentially good swings ruined when players use their arms to accelerate the club to the top of the backswing. This necessitates a tensing of the upper-body muscles to stop the backward momentum of the club. So the relaxed-arm key is lost and the swing is likely to fail.

Therefore, *it is imperative that the club move slowly as we finish the windup*. This applies not only to the basic arc, but to the full swing, which we will be discussing shortly.

The finish of the backswing and the beginning of the downswing can be considered together as *the change of direction*. In the change of direction the club will start down at the same speed it finished coming up: *slowly.* The vast majority of all good teachers and players agree that the change of direction is the *slowest* movement in the swing. Many go so far as to advocate a slight stop or pause at the change of direction.

The change of direction occurs slowly in the effortless swing for two reasons. First, we contract an entire set of muscles to coil the body and raise the club, then a different and opposing set of muscles must contract to uncoil the body. It takes a moment for the contracted muscles to relax and vice versa. Second, as we know, the downswing begins with the weight shift from the right pivot point to the left pivot point. This movement requires time to occur, and will move the club *slowly* into its downward arc, without any abrupt pulling by the arms.

Let me sum up this important point as follows: You cannot believe how slowly the arms can move in a good downswing.

Humming Versus the Grunt Reflex

It would seem as if a successful swing is guaranteed by a slow change of direction and a gradual buildup of momentum which feels as if it peaks in the follow-through. Indeed, success is virtually assured if we can just resist that well-known last-second urge to attack the ball as the club nears impact. I call this last bastion of the hit impulse the *grunt reflex,* which is the player's attempt to add a little (or a lot) more speed to the club by pushing the triangle or umphing the club into the ball. The primary symptoms of the grunt

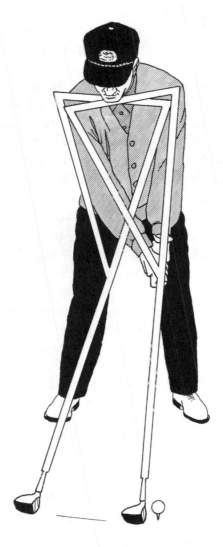

*Promote good rhythm — and a slower backswing — by making a connected, one-piece takeaway. Let the shoulders and torso move the **y** into the backswing arc.*

reflex are a sudden increase of grip pressure, a tensing of most of the upper body, and a last-instant push by the right hand. More often than not, the results are topped or fat shots.

We can overcome the grunt reflex and restore our effortless sensations with a simple technique: *humming* during the swing. The goal is to create the entire basic arc (or the full swing) while humming in a continuous monotone. At first, the grunt reflex will cut off the air flow, or cause the humming to become louder and more strained. Such results are a sure sign that the player is interfering with the natural buildup of momentum and trying to *hit* the ball. In short order, this humming technique will reduce and finally eliminate the grunt reflex, and the effortless swing will be a reality.

To sum up our discussion of good rhythm, we see that a one-piece takeaway, a slow change of direction, and a gradual increase in momentum (caused by the weight shift and uncoiling) will accelerate the arms and club through the ball position so that the fastest moment is sensed in the follow-through. The best sports analogy to this sensation I can offer is that of a discus thrower who unwinds, releases the discus, and perhaps feels as if his arm moves fastest as it extends into the follow-through.

We could justifiably assert that our final key, good rhythm, is a natural result of proper execution of the other keys. In fact, effortlessness is synonymous with good rhythm. The concept of our final key serves mainly as a feedback system to assess our success in utilizing the keys. If the rhythm is not good, we need to review the other swing keys.

Before we progress from the basic arc to the full swing, I request that you do yourself a favor and make many practice swings with the basic arc and no golf ball. *Then* hit shots with the basic arc on and off a tee. Everything you need to know has been presented.

If you are duffing or whiffing the ball, in most cases you are working too hard with the arms, or they are so tense they can't drop the **y** soon enough or low enough to reach the ball position. Occasionally, you may coil insufficiently or fail to shift the weight as suggested. A few golfers will be guilty of moving the swing center. The answers to any problems you may experience will become apparent as you watch yourself in the mirror and review this text.

More than likely, though, those who have come along this far will be experiencing tremendous success with the basic arc. If you are, go and practice what you are good at. Build the muscle memory and the instinctive feel and kinesthetic sense. Why bother rushing to hit balls with a full swing and a driver? That ability will be yours before long.

Instead, discipline yourself to practice using the basic arc to hit shorter shots of ten to fifty yards to specific targets until you are well skilled. Whether it takes a week or a month or two months, it will pay big dividends later on. So, put this book aside and master the basic arc through practice. Hundreds of players have succeeded at it, and you will too!

LESSON SIX
Expanding the Arc

The transition from the basic arc to the full swing is entirely a matter of arm bend and wrist action. The transition should be easily achieved, provided you have mastered shot-making with the basic arc.

Our goal is simply to increase clubhead speed by creating more centrifugal force than is possible with the basic arc. To achieve this, we will expand the swing arc by raising the club higher on the backswing and follow-through.

We lengthen the backswing arc mostly by bending the right arm, and we lengthen the follow-through arc mostly by bending the left arm. We create additional clubhead speed by allowing the wrists to hinge freely between the arms and club shaft, thereby dividing our arm-shaft lever and making two levers. This free hinging will enable our centrifugal force to impart additional speed to the clubhead as it approaches the ball.

As we begin to expand the arc, it becomes even

69

more essential to maintain relaxed, limber, *lightweight* arms. It is our intent to *have the body swing the arms along a greater arc,* not to let the arm motion overpower our basic sequence of moves. The arms remain basically subservient to the swing motions of the legs, hips, torso, and shoulders. They will swing freely up and down in the context of the coiling and uncoiling motion.

First, the Three-Quarter Swing

The easiest way to conceive and experience the proper up-and-down movement of the full swing is to start in the lighthouse-turn position, extending the **y** and the club straight out in front of the body, parallel to the ground. Now, keeping the left arm relatively straight, bend the right elbow into the chest and stomach. I hope you noticed that the wrists tend to hinge vertically at the base of the thumbs, until the club shaft is perpendicular to the ground, more or less parallel to the spine, and the club shaft and left arm form a 90-degree angle. The butt end of the grip points directly at the ground. If your spine is tilted just slightly forward, you can now make your lighthouse coil, and you will find you have created a three-quarter backswing.

You can also achieve the three-quarter position by making the backswing for the basic arc, then bending the right elbow into the body and allowing the wrists to hinge the club vertically. Of course, the arms remain relaxed and limber, and the left arm is extended but not necessarily locked.

To expand the basic arc to a three-quarter swing, bend the
right elbow in, toward the body, and allow the wrists to
hinge freely at the base of the thumbs. The result will be
a 90-degree wrist cock.

The Full Backswing

The transition to the full backswing is quite simple. From the three-quarter position, merely raise the arms higher, allowing the right elbow to move straight up and out from the body, and point the club shaft over your right shoulder toward the target. You will notice that the elements of the coil have not been affected: The left shoulder is fully coiled and the right pivot point is set.

The arc of the clubhead has been lengthened by virtue of the right arm bend, the concurrent raising of the extended left arm, and the vertical hinging of the wrists at the base of the thumbs.

If you have achieved this position correctly, the club shaft will rest on your left thumb. Your elbows will be fairly close together. The right elbow will point toward the ground. Raising the right elbow too high results in an overswing which sets up disconnection and the hit impulse. Neither does the right elbow move out toward the right side, pointing behind the player. This totally unnecessary movement creates distance between the elbows, flattens the left arm against the chest, and results in disconnection, shanks, slices, and occasional big hooks.

So one of the major elements of the proper full backswing will be *keeping the elbows in,* toward each other, not unlike our inward knee pressure. Maintaining close elbows decreases our chances of disconnecting and encourages our arms to swing in tandem with our body turn.

INCORRECT!
*Don't allow the right
elbow to move too far
out from the right side,
pointing behind you.*

*Expand the arc to a full swing by raising the left arm and
the right elbow a little higher. Note that the elbows work
better together when they remain relatively close together.
At the top of the backswing, the club rests on the left thumb.*

Let us now create the full backswing from the normal address position.

The "one-piece" coiling motion of the left shoulder, hip, and knee moves the **y** away from the ball. As the coiling continues, the right elbow begins to bend into the body. The **y** passes a point similar to the backswing position of the basic arc, but the right arm will be bent, and the wrists will be hinging the club vertically. As the shoulders complete the coiling motion and the right pivot point is set, the club shaft falls against the left thumb and *points toward the target.*

How Far Back?

At the completion of the full backswing, the club shaft may be parallel to the ground, but, *please,* take it no farther. The potential problems of an overswing far outweigh the possibility of slight gain in distance. In fact, for the vast majority of your golf shots, the ideal length of your backswing arc will be somewhere between the three-quarter and the full swing.

One element of the backswing is a little tricky. That is, I recommend that the upward movements of the arms be completed *at the same moment* as the coiling of the shoulders. This is not some esoteric theory I cooked up to complicate matters. Rather, this conclusion resulted from watching the many errors which occur when the arms continue to raise the club after the completion of the backswing turn.

The most frequent errors are overswinging and disconnection. In other cases, the continued raising of the arms will actually pull the spine out of position

Hale Irwin demonstrates the ideal full backswing. The club shaft is parallel to the ground, and points towards the target.

and tilt it toward the target. As a result, the weight remains on the left foot, and the downswing is likely to hit the ground many inches behind the ball. In other cases, the continued raising of the arms results in the acceleration of the club at the top of the swing, excess muscle tension, and the reflexive reaction—the hit impulse.

In short, the higher the club moves after the completion of the body coiling, the greater the likelihood of swinging down with only the arms instead of with a connected body motion. So, again, I suggest you endeavor to complete the raising of the arms and club and the hinging of the wrists at the same moment you complete the backswing turn. It may take a while to master it, but the dividends will be immense. This idea may help explain why players achieve better shot results when they "don't take it back as far."

A Vote for Passive Wrists

Before discussing the sequence of motion in the downswing, a few observations are warranted about the element of wrist action. I side with the majority (I believe) of instructors who advocate *passive wrists*. That is, the wrist joint at the base of the thumbs is completely free of tension, and simply responds to the forces created by the torso motion and arm swing.

Certainly, it is possible to willfully "lash" the wrists and clubhead into the impact zone. A few good players have done so. Yet, as we have noted, impact lasts about one two-thousandth of a second, and accurately timing such a wrist movement will be extremely difficult. In

Jack Nicklaus demonstrates "dropping it into the slot" (insert), and the feeling of powerful release.

fact, Alastair Cochran and John Stobbs in *The Search for the Perfect Swing* observe that deliberate wrist action will fail if it occurs one-seventieth of a second too early! Moreover, I feel the grunt reflex is often an expression of a player's attempt to add additional wrist action to the shot. This "willful release" slows the arms prematurely, creates a counterforce to our momentum, and results in an early release, and fat and thin shots.

Therefore, as we begin the downswing, the wrist joints remain relaxed and passive and the club continues to rest on the left thumb. As the right knee begins its movement toward the ball, to shift the weight to the left pivot point and begin the connected uncoiling motion, the right elbow merely drops into the body again and rides along momentarily with the uncoiling motion.

I emphasize this point because the movement is by no means natural and must be learned. The natural reaction, which unhappily is not the correct one, is for the buildup of centrifugal force to pull the arm and club away from the body as the downswing begins. Most bad players cooperate with this tendency by pushing the club out with the right arm—the classic "over the top" hit impulse and "early release."

So, again, I assert that as the weight shift initiates the downswing, the club continues to rest on the left thumb and the right elbow drops back into the body. Many golf enthusiasts refer to this movement as "dropping it into the slot." This movement separates the good players from the "earth movers," and is not a violent action. The term is not "jerk it into the slot," or jam it or pull it or yank it or shove it. Simply trust gravity and focus on *dropping* it into the slot. The feeling will be that the butt end of the club drops directly down toward the ball as the body begins to unwind. The club shaft still will be almost vertical to the ground.

Release!

At this point, the powerful momentum resulting from the weight shift and the uncoiling of the connected hips and torso should be the dominant sensation. The relaxed arms are literally being swung by the body. The player will feel as though the butt end of the club were falling toward the ball, and in the next instant the speed is sensed in the follow-through.

What has happened in the interim is that centrifugal force has traveled down the arms and into the shaft, and has caused the *release* of the 90-degree arm-shaft angle (wrist cock), pulling the weight of the club off the left thumb and accelerating the clubhead through the golf ball.

Again, the player does not initiate the release as an act of will. In fact, he or she is barely aware of it.

The release of the relaxed wrist cock occurs as a natural reaction to the buildup of centrifugal force in the swing. In a somewhat slow-motion swing, the club feels as if it merely *flops* through the impact zone. I cannot emphasize strongly enough the need for absence of tension and strain in the arm and wrist portion of the downswing. The arms and club fly through the ball position into a high, comfortable, balanced follow-through. *The grip pressure has not tightened* because there was no grunt reflex.

The other checkpoints of the full-swing follow-through are very similar to those of the basic arc. The weight is solid on the left foot. The right foot is straight up and down (on the toe). The knees are touching. The belt buckle faces the target, and is slightly ahead of the swing center. The chest faces just to the left of the target.

In the full swing, the club arms swing well past the finish point of the basic arc. The left arm bends as the right arm straightens into the follow-through, and the club continues along its arc over the left shoulder. If the wrist joint remains relaxed, it will be natural for the wrists to hinge again at the base of the thumbs.

In general, I do not advocate allowing the back of the left hand to collapse at the wrist in the follow-through, or anywhere else. The straight-line relationship between the back of the left hand and the left forearm should remain constant throughout the swing. Actually, the back of the left hand will rotate 90 degrees as the arms swing the club up and down in a **v** in front of the body as it turns. This movement occurs naturally and requires little attention by the player. Certainly, we have more than enough to think and feel!

LESSON SEVEN
The Inside-Out Swing

There is really nothing mysterious about the inside-out swing. The term "inside-out" refers to the direction the club shaft is moving as it approaches the ball on the downswing. "Inside" refers to the space on the player's side of the target line extending directly through the ball and target, to infinity in both directions. Everything on the far side of the target line is "outside."

To get a better image of "inside" and "outside," imagine a huge record disc, about ten feet in diameter. Picture the disc straight up and down (vertical to the ground) extending along the target line. One point along the edge of the disc touches the target line exactly at the ball position. Now assume your stance and tilt the album about 45 degrees until the hole in its center goes over your head. Now the center of the disc rests on your shoulders and its edge still touches the target line.

Imagine a huge record album to help you visualize the swing plane. During the swing, keep the club under, or inside the record album.

If you can visualize this, you will agree that the entire outside edge of the disc reasonably indicates the path of the clubhead during the swing, and the entire area of the disc reasonably describes our "swing plane." So let us say that the space under the disc represents "inside" the plane, and the space beyond the top of the disc represents "outside" the swing plane. This analogy isn't perfect, but it should be helpful to us.

As you can guess, a successful inside-out swing is achieved when the club stays along or under the record disc during the swing. As the clubhead approaches the ball, it *feels* to the player *as if* it is moving from inside toward outside the target line. It feels during the downswing as if the player is going to hit the ball well to the *right* of the intended target. This is quite natural. Actually, the turning of the torso and shoulders swings the club first from the inside toward outside, but as the turning continues, the club moves along the target line (through the ball) and then inside the target line again during the follow-through.

Thus the club never actually goes outside the target line, even though, again, it feels as if it swings down from inside to outside. When we feel "inside-out" we are actually swinging "inside-along-inside" the target line.

So I am insisting (assuming the shoulders, hips, and feet are aligned parallel to the target line) that to hit the ball down the target line, the player will feel as if he or she is swinging the club *down and out to the right of the target*. Again, the body turn will keep the club on the proper path. The majority of players will not agree with me at this point, because (unbeknownst to them) they are aligning to the right of the target and swinging outside-in, or "over the top," of the ideal plane to hit the ball to the target.

The Question of Timing

The keys already presented virtually ensure a correct inside-out (or "inside-to-inside," if you prefer) swing path, if the sequence of moves is timed properly. This reopens the delicate question of what moves first on the downswing. Does the body weight shift, or does the right elbow fall down into the right side, dropping the club into the slot? (Of course, most unskilled players fail to make either move and instead push the club away from the body with the right arm.)

I said before that the two moves occur virtually simultaneously. If the arms are relaxed, the driving of the right knee toward the ball will tend to drop the right elbow and club into the slot.

However, if you are pulling the ball to the left of your target, or slicing it, and your divots point considerably to the left of the target, you are swinging outside-in. In such cases, you will need to feel the arms drop into the slot sooner than you are at present, even (and I hate to say it) slightly before the weight shift. Most likely, you also need to relax your upper body, making it more willing to drop the arms without resistance. It may also help to delay the unwinding of your shoulders until you feel the arms begin to drop and the weight begin to shift. Remember, the shoul-

The club is likely to hit the ground at a point opposite your center of gravity. So, if your clubhead hits the ground behind the ball, your weight is probably still on your right foot. Shifting the weight to the left foot at the start of the downswing helps you to hit the ball before you make contact with the ground.

ders shouldn't begin to unwind until the hip motion pulls them. (I am assuming that you *are* coiling the left shoulder to a point above the right hip.)

On the other hand, if your divots point well to the right of the target, and the club hits the ground before it reaches the ball, you may be dropping your arms without creating sufficient momentum via the coil and weight shift. The club is likely to hit the ground at a point on the target line opposite your center of gravity. So, if your relaxed arms drop the club into the ground back by your right foot, most likely your weight is still on your right foot. In such a case, you may have failed to coil sufficiently into the right pivot point on the windup, so you were not in position to shift and uncoil; no momentum was created, and the uncoiling was never completed.

As we have seen, the concerted timing of the upper and lower body movements at the initiation of the downswing determines your degree of success in swinging inside-out. Let's hope your divots are pointing down the target line or only slightly to the left (or right) of it. To help you experience the inside-out swing, and to feel as if the club were swinging down and out to the right of the target, may I suggest that, for the time being, you endeavor to feel as if the downswing arc were slightly below, or inside, the backswing arc. In other words, make the downswing arc "flatter" or less upright than the backswing arc. And, in any event, keep it *under* the imaginary record disc.

If this suggestion fails to bring the desired results, retreat to a half or three-quarter swing, keeping the arms very relaxed, and the right elbow completely against the right side throughout the backswing and downswing. Assuming the keys have been correctly established, practicing this smaller swing will guarantee permanent success.

The Keys and the Course

These pages contain a great deal of information, for they are a distillation of a very complex subject. The basic theme has been to present as clearly and simply as possible the most efficient and effortless approach to creating momentum and clubhead speed in the swing.

The first step is to create good balance, primarily via inward knee pressure, with the weight on the inside edges of the feet. The next step is to create momentum via the elements of coiling, weight shift, and connection. Here I recommend paying considerable attention to efficient knee action. Third, we build a steady swing center to guarantee consistent shot-making. Fourth, we add the vertical element of swing arc via relaxed, subservient arm and wrist action. And, finally, the sensations are blended harmoniously to create good rhythm, with a feeling of speed in the follow-through.

Players vary in their ability to feel the swing motions. Some feel many distinct sensations; others start

89

Slammin' Sam Snead says, "My mind is blank and my body is loose as a goose." Build muscle memory so you, too, can play by feel.

the club, and zing, it's over. In any event, for most of us, a good swing should not feel fast. *I believe the dominant sensations should be the coiling, the setting of the pivot points, the relaxed arms, and the speed in the follow-through.*

As I have recommended many times, all these sensations can become reflexive through practice. When this occurs, the mind can be quite free from distinct thoughts, commands, or sensations. Instead, the player can anticipate the overall feeling of a good swing and wait while the body produces that swing. As Sam Snead says: "My mind is blank and my body is loose as a goose." At this point, an advanced skill level has been achieved.

The player then can focus more intensely on visualization and target orientation. He or she can anticipate, even feel, the initial trajectory of the shot, and see it fly to the target. With the trust that comes from practice, the player will patiently and effortlessly produce the desired swing. The rhythm-wrecking results of anxiety will occur infrequently. An attitude of positive expectancy will be achieved.

I recommend, therefore, that the reader commit to mastering the keys, one at a time, as they are presented. The greatest long-term benefit is that you will be freed from a constant search for a "tip" that works. Unlike the majority of players who spend their entire golf lives searching, experimenting, and analyzing, the player who builds the keys to the effortless swing will finally trust his or her swing and will be freed to play in the higher realm of visualization and anticipated feeling.

I wish you the greatest success!

Bibliography

Ballard, J. *How to Perfect Your Golf Swing*. New York: Simon and Schuster, 1981.

Boomer, Percy. *On Learning Golf*. New York: Alfred A. Knopf, 1977.

Cochran, Alastair, and John Stoobs. *The Search for the Perfect Swing*. Philadelphia and New York: J. B. Lippincott, 1968.

Geiberger, A., and L. Dennis. *Tempo—Golf's Master Key: How to Find It, How to Keep It*. New York: Simon and Schuster, 1980.

Hogan, B., and H. W. Wind. *Five Lessons—The Modern Fundamentals of Golf*. New York: A. S. Barnes, 1957.

Nicklaus, J., and K. Bowden. *Golf My Way*. New York: Simon and Schuster, 1974.

Snead, S., and L. Sheehan. *Sam Snead Teaches You His Simple "Key Approach to Golf."* New York: Atheneum, 1975.

MICHAEL MCTEIGUE, a native of New Jersey, now lives in Palo Alto, California. A Phi Beta Kappa graduate of UCLA with a degree in psychology and a recent M.B.A. from the Stanford University Graduate School of Business, McTeigue has conducted thousands of lessons as a golf professional at the Bel Air and Riviera country clubs and the Palos Verdes Golf Club.